MOUNTAIN VIEW SCHOOL DISTRICT

Rice Cakes
and
Paper Dragons

Rice Cakes
and
Paper Dragons

By SEYMOUR REIT

Photographs by PAUL CONKLIN

DODD, MEAD & COMPANY
New York

To my sister, Phyllis

The author wishes to express his deep appreciation to the family of Mr. and Mrs. Leslie Chan for their kind and unstinting cooperation during the creation of this book. He also wishes to thank, for their help and guidance, Mr. John Lee of the New York Chinese School; Miss Virginia Swift of the Chatham Square Branch of the New York Public Library; and Mr. Samuel Cooper, Principal of P.S. 65. Special thanks also go to Mr. Irwin B. Nelson for supplying the photographs which appear on pages 15, 20, 21, 23, 33, and 64, and to Mr. Tim Lew for the calligraphy on page 10.

Chart of Chinese calendar reproduced on page 9 copyright ©1972 by The New York Times Company. Reprinted by permission.

Contents

1

Eight Days to Go

Marie Chan looked up from the calendar she had just been studying. "Five days in January, and three days in February," she said. "That makes eight all together."

"What in the world are you talking about?" her brother Roland asked.

"I know," said Marie's older sister, Melissa. "She's been counting the days until New Year's."

Marie smiled, because Melissa had guessed it. Chinese New Year's was Marie's favorite holiday. This year it would fall on February third, which was eight days away.

Marie put the calendar down. Eight days seemed such a long time to wait. It would be a long while before she could shout, "Gung Ho Sun Hee!" which means "Happy New Year!" in Chinese. Before she could eat the little holiday rice cakes called *lin go,* and the delicious shrimp patties called *law par go.* Before she could listen to the firecrackers pop, and watch the paper dragons go parading through the streets. She could hardly wait to say good-by to the Year of the Mouse and hello to the Year of the Ox.

In school Marie has learned all about the Chinese calendar, which is quite different from the calendar of the Western world. According to an ancient legend, Lord Buddha once invited all the animals to a great meeting, but only twelve animals came. To honor these animals, Buddha named a special year after each one. This became the Chinese "twelve-year cycle."

The cycle begins with the Year of the Mouse. Next is the Year of the Ox. Then comes the Year of the Tiger, the

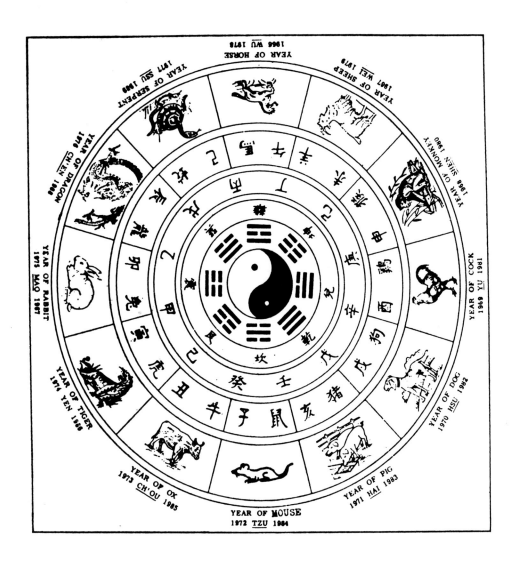

Rabbit, the Dragon, the Serpent, the Horse, the Sheep, the Monkey, the Cock, and the Dog. Last comes the Year of the Pig. Then the cycle starts all over again.

In eight days, the Year of the Ox would arrive. Marie had already decided that on New Year's Day she would use her Chinese name. Of course, she and her sisters and brother all had American names, and they used them almost all the time. But it is a tradition among Chinese-American parents to give their children Oriental names too. These are used on very special holidays. They also appear on official papers, such as school reports and marriage certificates.

Marie's Chinese name is Sook Hing. It means "Virtuous Fragrance." In Chinese writing it looks like this:

 Chan

Sook

Hing

Marie had been practicing how to write her Chinese name. After lunch she wrote it on a piece of paper, and showed it to Melissa.

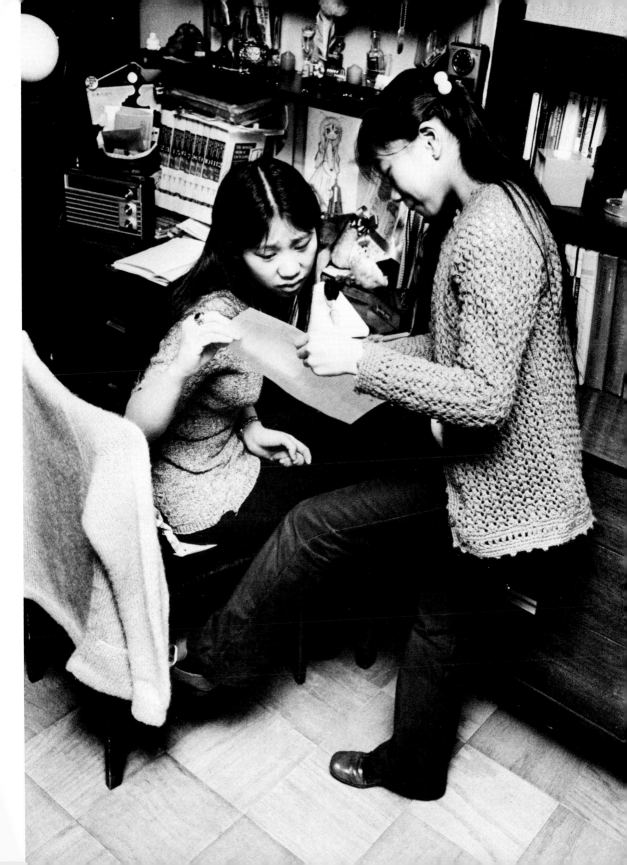

"All year long, I'm just plain ordinary Marie," she said. "But on New Year's Day I'm going to be Sook Hing. Everyone will have to call me Sook Hing. That's the custom."

Marie looked at the calendar again and sighed. Calendars never change their minds. No matter how many times she counted, she knew it would come out the same. The New Year's holiday was still eight days away. And right now, to Marie, eight days seemed almost as long as forever.

2

All Around Chinatown

The next day was Saturday, and since there was no school, Marie went shopping with her mother. The neighborhood where Marie lives is called Chinatown.

Chinatown is almost a complete little world in itself. But it is a very special world, because it is right in the middle of a huge city — the city of New York!

Marie's neighborhood has almost everything a big city has. There are Chinese newspapers and Chinese movie theaters. There is a Chinese radio station. There are Chinese tea shops and clothing shops. There are Chinese banks and book shops. There are Chinese beauty parlors and grocery stores. There are twelve churches

in Chinatown, and two Buddhist temples. Even the telephone booths on the street corners look like little Chinese pagodas.

The Chinese people first came to this part of New York in the 1840's. In those days, America's great railroads were being built. But building a railroad takes many strong backs and hands. Thousands of Chinese laborers were

brought to the United States, to help pound the heavy wooden ties and lay the long steel rails.

When the railroads were finally finished, some Chinese stayed on the West Coast. But others came east to New York. They settled in lower Manhattan, to earn their living and raise their families.

As the years passed, more and more Chinese families came. Their little "city within a city" grew and grew. Today more than 60,000 people live in the area, and almost all are Chinese.

Marie's mother was born in New York. Her father was born in Canton, China, and came to America as a young man. Some Chinese-Americans are Buddhists, but most belong to the Christian faith. The Chan family attends a Lutheran church in the neighborhood.

The people here work at all kinds of jobs and professions. There are painters and plumbers. And doctors and lawyers. And schoolteachers and truck drivers. And nurses and musicians. And shopkeepers and housewives and dentists and school children.

The people of Chinatown like their special world. But they also like being part of the larger world of New York and of America. And they take pride in being American citizens. Along with the Chinese signs on the storefronts, there are many signs in English. And on the newsstands there are American newspapers right next to the Chinese ones.

The main streets of Marie's world are called Mott Street and Pell Street. Here there are many fine restaurants. People come to these restaurants from all over the city to enjoy delicious Chinese meals. There are also many curio shops, where one can buy fans and kimonos and small ivory carvings and beautiful jade jewelry. And there are food markets which sell Chinese delicacies such as bamboo shoots, water chestnuts, dried duck, bean sprouts, and lichee fruit.

Most of the buildings in Chinatown are small and very old, since they were built a great many years ago. But Marie lives in a large modern apartment building on Bayard Street. She lives there with her father and mother, her brother Roland, and her sister, Melissa. Another sister, Rosanne, is studying to be a nurse. Rosanne stays at a nurses' dormitory, and only comes home on weekends. She also sings in the Lutheran Church choir.

When Marie got home from her shopping trip, she looked at the calendar again. "Another day gone," she thought. "Now there are seven."

During the night she had a strange dream. She dreamed

that she was walking along Mott Street when a huge paper dragon called a Foo Dog suddenly appeared. It was the kind of dragon that always dances in the streets on New Year's Day. In her dream, Marie climbed on the dragon's back, and off they galloped. After a while, the huge beast began to fly. It circled high above the narrow streets of Chinatown, with Marie clinging to its back. Soon the Foo Dog began to twist and buck. Marie started to shake and bounce, but she held on tightly. The shaking grew worse and worse, and Marie was afraid that she would fall off. Then she opened her eyes — and there was her mother shaking her by the shoulder.

"Wake up, Marie," said Mrs. Chan, "or we'll be late for church."

3

More than One School

The days before New Year's passed slowly for Marie. Like children all over America, she goes to school five days a week. From nine o'clock in the morning until three o'clock in the afternoon. Marie's school is P.S. 65. It is only a few blocks from home, so she can walk there easily.

Most of the boys and girls in Marie's class are Chinese. But there are some white children and black children too. Their teachers are Mrs. Schecter and Mr. Whitman. The subjects for this year are English, Science, Math, Social Studies, French, and Home Economics.

Marie's favorite is Social Studies. In Social Studies the children learn about people of other lands. This week

they were studying Brazil. Marie learned that the people of Brazil speak a language called Portuguese, and that everyone drinks strong coffee from little cups. Even the children! She learned that there are vast jungles in Brazil, filled with wild animals and beautiful plumed birds. There are many parrots in the Brazilian jungles. Marie remembered once seeing parrots in a pet shop on Doyers Street.

During recess, everyone goes to the schoolyard to play games and gossip with friends. Marie's best friend is a girl named Louise.

In the yard, the children play the same kinds of games that children play everywhere. The most popular game is "Johnny-Ride-the-Pony."

School is out at three o'clock. But that isn't the end of Marie's school day. Every afternoon, for two more hours, Marie attends a special Chinese class. It is held in the Chinese Community Center, around the corner from her home.

Many other Chinese-American children attend this special school. Here, they all use their Chinese names.

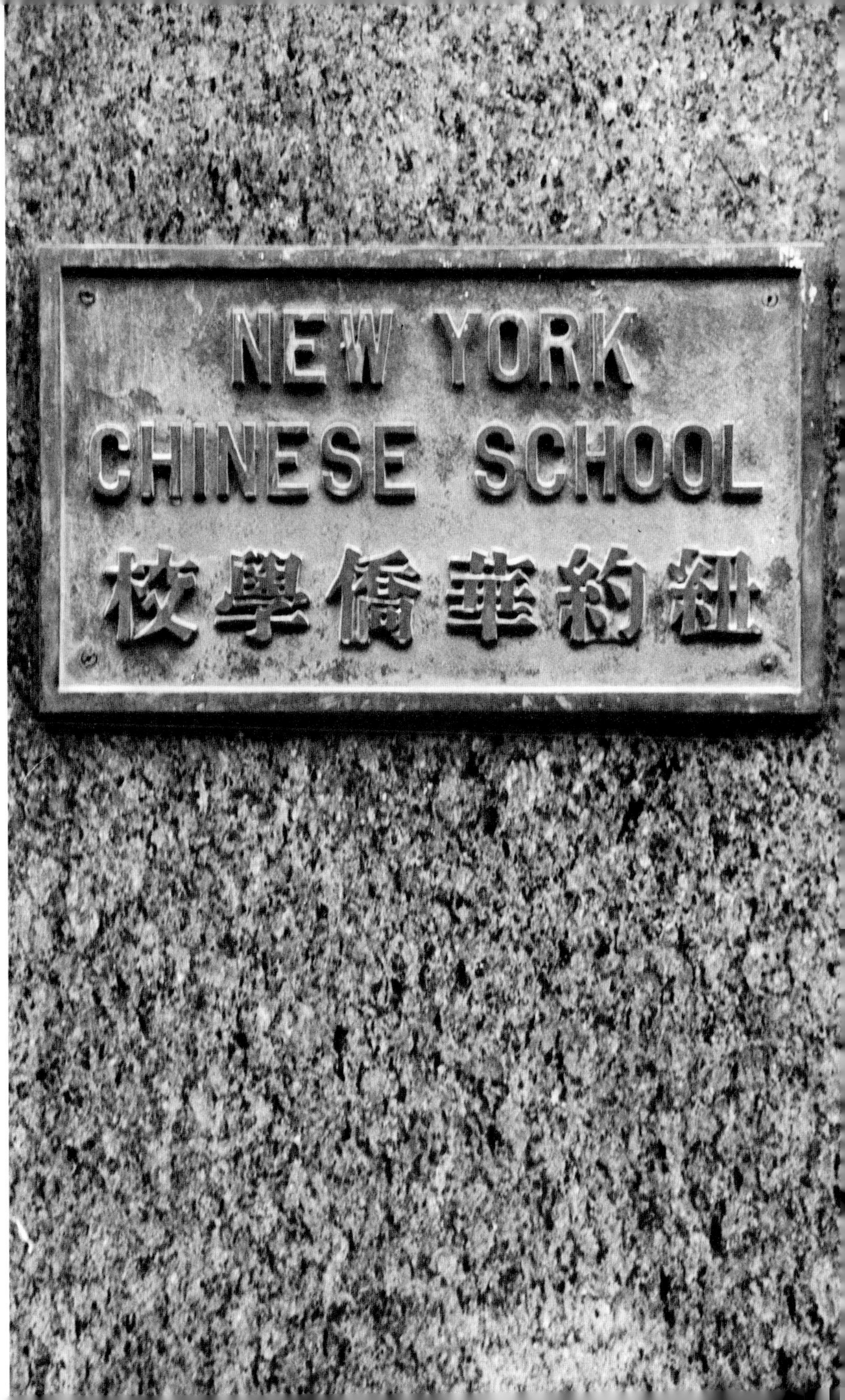
NEW YORK
CHINESE SCHOOL
紐約華僑學校

Their teacher, Mr. Lee, teaches them how to read and write the Chinese language. They also learn about Chinese art, music, history, and customs. And sometimes Mr. Lee reads Chinese folk tales to them.

Marie likes the writing lessons best of all. Chinese isn't written with a pen, but with a special kind of brush. And the writing goes up and down, instead of from side to side. Marie is learning to write the strange letters by tracing them from a book. Chinese is hard to write, but

beautiful to look at. To Marie, the characters are just like tiny dancers, leaping and whirling over the white pages.

Chinese school gives the children of Chinatown a link between the past and the present. From Mr. Lee, Marie and the others have learned about the great ruling families

of ancient China, called "dynasties." They have learned about the Han dynasty, which was devoted to peace and brotherhood. And about the Sung dynasty, which was a time of progress in art and poetry. They have learned about the great emperor of the Yuan dynasty, Kublai Khan, who was visited by the famous Marco Polo.

Mr. Lee has also told them about the Great Wall of China. It was built during the Ming dynasty, almost 600 years ago, to keep out invading armies. The Great Wall is 25 feet high, and runs for 1500 miles along China's northern border. And to this day, most of it is still standing!

Long ago, on a trip to China, Mr. Lee saw the Great Wall himself. Marie thought that someday she would like to see it too.

4

A Chinese Guitar

At seven o'clock, when Marie gets home from Chinese school, the whole family sits down to dinner. Everyone helps with the dishes afterward, because Mrs. Chan has no time to waste. Her uncle, Tam Bing Yung, owns a busy restaurant in Chinatown. In the evenings, Mrs. Chan often goes to the restaurant to help Uncle Yung.

Sometimes Mrs. Chan's brother Charles comes to dinner. Uncle Charles teaches art in a New York high school. He is not only a good painter, but a fine sculptor as well. Now and then, Marie visits Uncle Charles in his studio. He shows her his work, and talks to her about the old ways.

Once he explained to Marie how the ancient Chinese believed that everything in the universe came in fives. The five colors were blue, yellow, red, white, and black. The five musical notes were do, re, mi, sol, and la. The five tastes were sweet, sour, bitter, pungent, and salt. To this day, at feast times, Marie's mother prepares meals that use all five of these tastes.

On some nights, Marie likes to sit and listen to her father play music. During the day Mr. Chan works as a machinist in a factory uptown. But in his spare time he plays in a Chinese orchestra. The orchestra performs at Chinese operas. It also gives concerts of Oriental music.

Mr. Chan plays many kinds of Oriental stringed instruments. His favorite is a guitar called a *san hsien*. He also plays the Chinese harp, the Chinese cello, and a little round instrument called a *yueh chin,* which means "moon guitar."

Chinese music began in the Shang dynasty, more than 3000 years ago. In those days, the Chinese believed that music had magic power over the elements. They felt that it could tame wild storms, and calm angry waves. Their music is very slow and gentle. It is much different in rhythm and tone from the music of the Western world.

When he plays the *san hsien* for Marie, Mr. Chan sometimes sings her an old Oriental song:

> A gentle wind fans the calm night;
> A bright moon shines on the tall tower . . .

Listening to the gentle music, and her father's soft voice, always makes Marie feel calm and peaceful.

5

A Ride on a Ferry

The Chan family is very much a part of the world of Chinatown. But they are also part of the larger world around them. As often as they can, the Chans take their children to visit other parts of the city.

Because of the coming holiday, Chinese school closed a few days early. So Mrs. Chan decided to take Marie on a ferry ride to Staten Island. Marie was excited because she had never been on a ferry ride before. Melissa came along too.

The Staten Island ferries go back and forth across New York Bay. The fare is ten cents, and the boat ride lasts about half an hour. Mrs. Chan and the girls took a bus

to the ferry slip at the southern end of Manhattan. It was a good day for an outing. There was a cool breeze, but the wintry sun was cheery and bright.

A squat little ferry was just nudging into the slip as the bus pulled up. Marie, Melissa, and Mrs. Chan dropped their dimes in the slots and hurried through the turnstiles. Their ferry was named the *Cornelius G. Kolff*. Its name was painted in bright gold letters on the pilot house.

"Wow!" said Melissa. "What a big name for such a little boat!"

The ferry had an odd shape. It was wide in the middle and round at both ends. And there was room on the bottom deck for automobiles.

With a blast of its whistle, the good ship *Cornelius G. Kolff* pushed bravely out into the bay. The girls stood at the ferry rail, their hair flying in the breeze. There was so much to see that Marie didn't know where to look first. Boats of all shapes and sizes moved through the bay. There were fussy little tugboats and rusty old oil tankers. There were cargo ships and coal barges. There were garbage scows and pleasure boats. There was even a huge oceanliner with red and white funnels, just setting out on a sea voyage.

Marie gripped Melissa's arm and pointed. "Look!" she said. "There's the Statue of Liberty!"

Mrs. Chan gave Marie a coin, and she put it in a telescope mounted near the railing. Through the telescope the statue seemed very close — almost close enough for Marie to touch.

There it stood on its huge pedestal, one arm carrying a book and the other holding a great torch. Marie remembered studying about the Statue of Liberty in school. She thought of all the millions of people — people like her very own father — who had been welcomed by the statue when they first came to live in America.

The ferry ride went quickly, and before they knew it they were docking at Staten Island. Most of the people got off and hurried away, but Mrs. Chan and the girls stayed on board for the return trip.

As the ferry started back again, a flock of gray seagulls circled overhead. They swooped back and forth, loudly scolding the people below.

Awk! Awk! Awk!

"Those birds sound angry," Marie said.

"They're not angry, just *hungry*." Melissa replied. "And so am I."

There was a refreshment stand in the passenger lounge. Mrs. Chan and the girls went inside, and everyone had hot dogs and soda. Then they all went out on deck again.

The girls walked up to the very front of the ferry. From here, they could watch the skyscrapers of Manhattan as the boat drew closer and closer.

Marie stared at the city skyline. She tried to find China-town, but it was hidden far behind the tall buildings. From the boat, the huge skyscrapers looked like toy blocks — the kind she had played with as a little girl. But these blocks were certainly a lot bigger. They reached up and up like the fingers of a great stone giant, trying to brush away the passing clouds.

Now the sun was ready to set. The wind whipped across the bay, and the air grew cold. Marie shivered inside her coat. She was glad when the ferry docked at last and she could climb aboard the warm bus for the ride back to Bayard Street.

That night Marie felt very tired. Her stomach hurt and she hardly ate any dinner. Mrs. Chan looked worried. She felt Marie's forehead and sent her off to bed early.

Mr. Chan took down his *san hsien* and began to tune the strings. "I think," he said, "that Marie has had too much ferry today."

6

Gloom and Doom

The next morning, Marie felt even worse. Mrs. Chan took her temperature.

"It's pretty high," she said. "I'd better call Dr. Shin."

When Dr. Shin arrived, he examined Marie carefully. He took her temperature again and felt her pulse. He looked down her throat. He listened to her chest with a stethoscope.

"Just a virus," he said to Marie's mother. "Nothing to worry about. But we have to be careful. There's a lot of this going around. Keep her in bed for a few days, and then we'll see."

When Marie heard that, her heart sank. A few days!

And New Year's only two days away! She couldn't miss the celebration. She just *couldn't!*

"I won't stay in bed," she wailed to her mother after the doctor had gone. "I'll miss all the fun."

Mrs. Chan shook her head. "I'm sorry, young lady. Your health comes first. You'll do just what the doctor tells you." She left the room, shutting the door firmly behind her.

Marie buried her head in the pillow. What a silly time to get sick! All her waiting, all her counting the days had been for nothing. She was going to miss the most im-

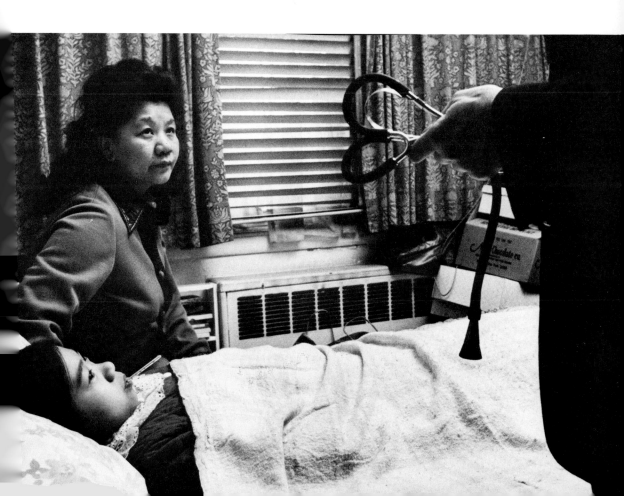

portant event of the whole year. And all because of a ferry ride.

Later, Marie got out of bed and looked forlornly out the window. She could see Mr. and Mrs. Wong, who owned a curio shop across the street. They were hanging bright red banners over the shop windows, getting ready for New Year's. Other people were also putting out flags and decorations. *Everyone* was getting ready for the holiday. And she was going to miss it all. She crept back to bed, feeling worse than ever.

During the afternoon, Roland poked his head into the room. He was carrying a little book wrapped in gold paper. "Hi," he said. "Here's something to cheer you up."

Marie took the gift and tried to smile. But she couldn't. She was just too miserable. She felt as though she would never ever smile again. Never, as long as she lived.

7

Getting Ready

When Marie woke up on Friday, her first thought was, one more day to go! Then she remembered, and her spirits drooped. What difference did it make *now?* Nothing mattered any more. Everyone would be out celebrating, and she would be home in bed. Imagine being sick on New Year's! Marie rolled over and covered her head with the blankets.

But as the day went on, she began to feel better and better. And more like her usual self. She even ate a good lunch. Maybe. Just maybe . . .

"Your temperature's almost normal," her mother said, reading the thermometer. "Let's wait and see what the doctor says."

When Dr. Shin came, he examined Marie again. Then he stroked his chin and looked thoughtful. What would he decide? Would he make her stay in bed? Marie held her breath.

"Well, if her temperature stays down," he finally said to Mrs. Chan, "I think she can go out for awhile to-morrow. But make sure she dresses warmly."

Marie broke into a big grin. The world suddenly looked bright again. Sook Hing would have her special day after all.

That evening Mrs. Chan finished her work in the kitchen, getting the last things ready for the festivities. The whole family helped. And mother's friend, Claire,

came over to lend a hand. They made holiday dishes and treats which they would serve on New Year's day.

They prepared a chicken, which would be cooked later

with Chinese mushrooms, ginger, and soy sauce. This dish is called *jung wat gai.* They made the traditional little rice cakes called *lin go,* which everyone eats on New Year's. They made patties called *law par go,* filled with shrimp, pork, and turnips. They filled a bowl with *loong lan,* which is fresh lichee fruit.

Melissa went out and bought a box of sweet pastries called *gin du yah.* She also brought back a big bag of oranges. It is a Chinese tradition to give oranges for good luck when you visit people on New Year's day.

Another custom is to give little gifts of money, wrapped

in bright red paper. Marie and Melissa wrapped quarters, fifty-cent pieces, and dollar bills in the red paper. Tomorrow they would give them to their friends and relatives. And they would get similar packets in return.

The others were still working when Marie went off to bed. She slid beneath the covers contentedly. The day had started out gloomily. Then everything had suddenly changed. And now she was ready for tomorrow.

8

Gung Ho Sun Hee!

Pop! Crack!

Marie opened her eyes. She sat up in bed and listened carefully.

Crack! Poppity-pop!

There it was again. The popping of firecrackers. New Year's was here at last! Even this early, people were out in the streets, setting off fireworks to welcome the Year of the Ox.

Rubbing sleep from her eyes, Marie hurried into the kitchen. Mrs. Chan was at the stove, and Roland was eating breakfast.

"Hi, Marie," he said. "Happy New Year!"

"Today," she replied loftily, "I'm not Marie. I'm Sook Hing."

"Okay, Sook Hing — but you *still* have to wash your face and brush your teeth," her mother said. "Then come have your orange juice."

Marie's fever was gone and she felt fine. She gulped her breakfast and hurried to dress. Melissa, sleepy-eyed, poked her head around the doorway.

"What's the big rush?" she asked. "The dragons won't be out before eleven."

"Well, I want to go out early so I won't miss anything," Marie answered.

"Okay. Give me a few minutes and I'll go with you."

The two girls hurried outside and headed toward Mott

Street. The air was crisp and the sun was shining — perfect weather for New Year's. Nearby, a little girl threw a firecracker. It arched into the street and went off with a loud *bang!* Now firecrackers were going off everyplace.

In New York, fireworks are against the law. But for this one day the police allow them in Chinatown. Chinese firecrackers are really quite small, but they make a great deal of noise.

Marie and Melissa walked past a Buddhist storefront temple. People were going inside to light incense sticks, and to pray for good luck during the coming year. Everyone is welcome in the temple, even those who are not Buddhists. So Marie and Melissa went inside.

In a corner of the temple there was a big red barrel filled with slips of rolled up pink paper. This was the "fortune barrel." Marie put a coin in the charity box and picked her fortune. She unrolled it and read the words:

> Jade of green,
> Rubies of red —
> Much joy will be yours
> In the days ahead.

"That," said Melissa, patting her sister, "is a neat way to start the year, Sook Hing."

Outside there was a bustle and a murmur from the crowd. "The dragon is coming!" a small boy shouted.

The girls ran out to see. Down the street it came — a great blue and silver beast made of wire, cloth, and paper, with a tossing head and a long flowing tail. The colorful head was held up by a young man underneath. He was dressed all in black. Another young man in black held the thrashing tail.

The dancer holding the head strutted and pranced in a grotesque way. The steps of the dragon dance are very traditional. They have been done just this way for many, many years. The boys who do the dancing go to a special class at the Chinese School to learn the ancient movements. And only the best ones are chosen to perform on New Year's.

Slowly, the colorful beast moved down the street. Behind it came a group of people in costumes, carrying blue and silver banners. Some were beating huge drums. Others were clashing brass cymbals.

In the Western world, dragons have always been looked on as frightening and dangerous creatures. But the Chinese believe that dragons are symbols of happiness and good luck. Their job, on New Year's Day, is to frighten away any evil spirits left behind by the old year.

The drums and cymbals kept up a loud, steady rhythm. Firecrackers popped noisily, sending up little puffs of smoke. The blue dragon bowed and circled. Its head bobbed. Its huge eyes rolled. Its mouth opened wide, showing a bright red tongue. Marie watched with delight.

"Look!" Melissa cried.

From the other direction came a second dragon. This one was gold, green, and yellow. "It's the Foo Dog!" some-one said. The beasts all had special names, such as Foo Dog, Chinese Bear, and Little Dragon. Followed by drum beaters and spear carriers, they wandered in and out of the streets of Chinatown.

Now and then two of the beasts would meet. Sometimes the animals would be friendly. They would bow politely to each other, and strut back and forth in a dignified man-ner. At other times they would be in a fighting mood.

The dragons would lunge at each other, tossing their heads angrily. Each one would try to outdo the other in courage and fierceness, hoping to impress the crowd.

By now the noise was almost deafening. It was so loud that many of the onlookers had to cover their ears. Marie covered her ears too. At the corner, the girls met their parents. They all moved with the crowd, trying to talk above the sound of the drums, cymbals, and fireworks.

Everywhere people bowed and said, "Gung Ho Sun Hee!" which is the customary New Year's greeting. And "Ho Sai Guy!" which means "Good luck!"

After a while, Mr. Chan herded the family into a tea shop for lunch. Marie ate quickly. Then she hurried out again to watch the festivities. A group of dancers was

giving a performance in front of the Community Center. The young men and women wore colorful robes and sashes. They did traditional Chinese dances such as the Sword Dance and the Ribbon Dance, moving in slow patterns to the beat of drums and cymbals.

During the afternoon the Chans began visiting their friends and relatives. Then they went home to greet their own guests. In the Chan apartment, people came and went, bringing oranges and little gift packets of money. Marie's friend Louise came. And Mrs. Chan's Uncle Yung. And Claire and Uncle Charles and many others.

They sampled the *lin go* and the *law par go* and all the other delicacies. They wished one another good luck and happiness. Marie played the piano. Mr. Chan played Chinese music on the *san hsien*. Then the remaining guests sat down to a festive dinner. Dishes piled with food were placed in the center of the table. Using chopsticks, they all helped themselves. Excited, Marie ate a lot of everything. She ate until she couldn't manage another mouthful.

It was late by the time dinner ended, and Marie felt very tired. "Time for you to be in bed," her mother said. She walked Marie to the bedroom door.

Marie yawned sleepily. "Good night, mother. I had a wonderful time." Mrs. Chan smiled. "I'm so glad. Good night, Sook Hing. And sleep well."

Inside her room, Marie took out her little pink fortune paper and read it again:

> Jade of green,
> Rubies of red —
> Much joy will be yours
> In the days ahead.

Well, Marie didn't know what kind of days were really ahead for her. But she did know *one* thing. This particular day had been just about perfect.

The Author

SEYMOUR REIT, a native New Yorker, is the author of some twenty-five children's books. He is currently associated as writer and editor with the Bank Street College of Education, and is a contributing author to the Encyclopedia Britannica Pre-school Library.

After graduation from New York University, Mr. Reit started his career as an animator of films, and created the popular television character, "Casper the Friendly Ghost." During World War II he served as a captain on the personal staff of General Hoyt Vandenberg (9th Air Force) and experienced the European campaign from invasion through VE Day. Later he turned to writing — advertising, radio, television, documentary films, and books for young readers. He is married, lives in Manhattan, and has appeared for many years on "Around the Corner," a televised program sponsored by the New York City Board of Education.

The Photographer

PAUL CONKLIN is a free-lance photographer and writer now living in Washington, D.C. Assignments, as a Peace Corps photographer and on his own, have taken him throughout the world. His pictures have appeared in *Life, Time, Vogue,* and *National Geographic,* as well as in textbooks and encyclopedias.

Mr. Conklin holds a B.A. degree in journalism from Wayne State University and an M.A. in history from Columbia University. He took photographs on the Navajo Reservation for CHILD OF THE NAVAJOS by Seymour Reit, and has written his own photographic book, CIMARRON KID.